Azim Premji

The mantra of Azim Premji, the Chairman of Wipro, is 'Ordinary people are capable of extraordinary things. Have the courage to think big.' This Azim Premji closely follows in life.

Azim Premji's full name is Azim Hashim Premji. His father's name was M.H. Hasham Premji. He comes from a rich entrepreneur family. His grandfather was the rice king of Burma.

He was born on Mumbai, on July 24, 1945. His father belonged to a Gujarati Khoja Ismaili

Azim Premji

Premji with wife Yasmeen

Shia Muslim family. He was a leading rice merchant and a commission agent in Mumbai. In 1945, he started the Western India Vegetable Product Company which was later on called Wipro Limited. The company made hydrogenated vegetable oils and fats. Mohammed Ali Jinnah invited Hasham Premji to join the Muslim League in 1944. However, he declined owing to some personal and business reasons. He was again invited by Jinnah to join as the finance minister in the first cabinet of Pakistan. Premji's father refused to go to Pakistan and stayed on in India.

Azim Premji attended St Mary's school, I.C.S.E. Mazagaon, Mumbai. He completed his initial studies from St. Mary's and then he went to the USA. There he took admission in Stanford University, California, USA. He had selected a course in electrical engineering. He had not finished his undergraduate studies when his father passed away

With elder son Rishad Premji

suddenly. He was forced to discontinue his studies and came back to look after his father's company, which he now owned. Therefore, in 1966, at the age of twenty-one he took charge of the family business.

Considering his young age the shareholders at the first general meeting doubted his ability to handle the 2 million worth business his father had left and advised him to sell off his shares. They thought it befitting that he should leave the management of the company to more mature hands. However, not to be deterred by these suggestions, Azim Premji resolved to make a success of the legacy left by his father. He was

With former President of India Dr. A.P.J. Abdul Kalam

determined to make it a success. He had a vision, a simple one; he wanted to build the company on a foundation of strong values.

Since his engineering studies had been cut short, he sought permission to take correspondence art courses and completed his bachelor's degree in Electric Engineering.

Premji started off with a simple vision: to build an organization on a foundation of values. He eventually received permission to take correspondence art courses to complete the requirements for his bachelor's degree in Electrical Engineering. After a gap of over thirty years he completed his study and took degree in Electrical Engineering. This shows his determination to achieve what he had set his mind to attain.

After the death of his father when Azim Premji took over, the company was dealing in only hydrogenated cooking oils and fats but later on through sheer grit and vision he diversified into bakery fats, toiletries

Receiving Padam Bhushan award from the then President of India, Smt Pratibha Patil

based on ethnic ingredients and baby toiletries. Then he diversified into totally different sectors. He embarked on an ambitious phase of expansion and diversification. In collaboration with General Electric, the company started manufacturing light bulbs. The company further diversified into other consumer products including soaps, baby care

Indian Business Tycoons, (sitting from left) – Azim Premji, Indira Nooyi, Deepak Parekh, (standing from left) – Sunil Mittal, Kumar Manglam Birla, Peter Sandz and Anshu Jain

products, shampoos, powders etc. Soon Wipro started a unit for manufacturing hydraulic cylinders and truck tippers. But Premji grew more ambitious and the next phase was entry into computer hardware. Gradually it entered the Information Technology (IT) field. Now Wipro made a foray into software development and medical systems, technology products and consumer items with offices worldwide.

From a company dealing in just edible oils and fats Premji transformed it into one of software technology – the need of the hour. He has kept pace with the growing demand of the world and today his

Premji with IACT team inaugurating a mission

company is a name in itself and is the largest independent Research and Development (R&D) service providers in the world. The company was one of the largest IT services in the world and pioneer in IT outsourcing, before it embarked in R&D services. It then started Product Engineering Services (PES), which dealt with outsourcing and off shoring of the R&D services. It also started Business Process Outsourcing (BPO) which was outsourcing of front and back office business functions including contact centre operations, accounting and human resource related processes to a third party.

Premji had a vision to build the company on a new level and the shift

Premji presenting a medal

from oils and soaps to IT and software was a calculated and focused one. He had inherited a company worth 2 million dollars and he took it to many billions. He has achieved what he had envisioned. However he is constantly diversifying in new fields.

This success has no effect on Premji on the personal front. He is a simple person with no pretentiousness. In fact he is media-shy, always maintaining a low profile. It is his work that speaks for him. Each success is taken by him in his stride not affecting his life style. In spite of the company being worth billions and he himself considered one of the richest men in the world, he still travels like any other man that is in economy class. Besides this he prefers staying at guest houses or budget hotels than in five star luxuries.

One can describe his lifestyle as legendary in simplicity. The legendary person – Azim Premji – is a person who shuns anything that is remotely flamboyant. He prefers things made in India. His clothes, watches and cars are all of Indian make. One can rightly say that he is Indian to the core. Not giving much importance to his own personal wealth and person he would rather talk about his own companies and the Indian business scenario. Thus he diverts attention from his individual self to larger issues in life. He has remained focused down the years. His focus is on the expansion of the company, the welfare of the employees, India as a whole and diversifying in various upcoming fields rather than his own personal wealth. Therefore he does not give importance to his own image building or his personal image. These are secondary to his corporation. This makes him an individual worth emulating. He is a man

Premji with Pillars of Wipro Mr. Girish Parajape (left) and Suresh Vasvani (right)

Premji with Chief of GE Group Jeffrey Immelt

who stands apart from the ordinary man. These are the qualities of a true pioneer — a celebrity.

Premji's inclination towards IT is very strong. When IBM left India in 1980, Azim Premji acted fast, finding it a golden opportunity to enter into computer business before any other Indian company. He hired the best engineers to develop computers. He is aware that in order to forge ahead in the present time one needs a strong basic knowledge of the IT world. Keeping this in mind he stepped into the competitive world of IT much before the others and made his mark or rather his company's mark

During the release of the book 'Jalebi Management' in Bengaluru

in it. Acknowledging the importance of information technology in life he advocates its use at all levels. He knows that if one has to progress in life and not lag behind one should be well versed in the present age technologies. Keep abreast with the time. What better way to do so than to acquire skills of the age. The present age is of technologies and society should accept it in order to keep pace with the world. He, therefore, is constantly forging ahead in the IT field. He knows that Indians are very good in this field and he, in his own way, is encouraging the emerging IT professionals in this field.

At one of the international conferences in Bangalore he

Premji with Shri Amit Mitra, Finance Minister of West Bengal

acknowledged the contribution of IT in earning respect in the world. According to him India today is not a country known for just snake charmers but a land of leaders in Information Technology (IT). Indians are spread all over the world excelling in IT. They are successful entrepreneurs in this field being recognized for their contributions.

His company recruits young students from five business schools in India. They recruit young MBAs who are at par with IIMs. The brightest are recruited. Then they train internally those who are promising but not of top level. They also recruit from other competitors or other industries. Besides this they also recruit from outside. These recruitments are done on the basis of criteria they have formed. The person should be able to work in all environments, be adaptable,

Premji with the then Chief Minister of Karnataka Shri Yadiyurppa

comfortable in ambiguous situations and the most important of all is that they should be able to adjust and reach the goal in specific time.

Premji's success and prominence is owing to his knowledge, foresight and planning, coupled with determination and perseverance. He would rather wait than bribe in order to get things done. Determined and steadfast he is also a workaholic who believes in working to survive and be successful in the present day competitive world.

He is also a strict employer who expects high degree of competence and honesty from his employees. There is no room for deception and lies. He is a man of principles. He is very strict and does not waver from his principles. He does not let off errors easily. Once when a general manager

Attending a convocation ceremony

Receiving life time achievement award

in his company made an inflated bill he gave him the marching order though his contribution to the company had been significant. It was a solitary lapse but he was not forgiven, because according to Premji it was a matter of principles and he never compromised on it. The code of conduct that he has set for his employees is – not to do anything that the media may print next day with their photograph. This is to be followed strictly and no concession is given to one who forgets it.

Azim Premji established, the Wipro Equity Reward Trust in 1984. This allows employees to hold shares in the company. In case of a mishap, retirement or disability the shares are transferred to the legal heirs or held by the employee depending on the case. This is to be decided within 90 days of the incident.

Premji is a family man. His family consists of his wife – Yasmeen and two children – Rishad and Tariq. Rishad works in the USA for GE and is married to Aditi. His second son Tariq has co-founded a dotcom and works from Bangalore.

Azim Premji has two hobbies — hiking and reading. He has another interest close to his heart and that is philanthropy. He established Azim Premji Foundation, a nonprofit organization for the education of children. This organisation has a vision of promoting quality primary

With Deputy Chairman of Planning Commission Shri Montek Singh Ahluwalia

education for children in order to uplift the society making it fair, equitable, humane and sustainable. This foundation formed in 2001, works in 13 states across India. It was funded solely by him. He is a rare entrepreneur who believes in philanthropy. According to him even if he gave his children a part of his wealth it would be sufficient for them. Therefore, he prefers like Bill Gates to give away his money during his lifetime.

Premji has been conferred many honours and awards. Business Week recognized him as one of the Greatest Entrepreneurs. The Manipal

With Shri N.R. Narayana Murthy of Infosys

Academy of Higher Education, in 2000 conferred an honorary doctorate. In 2005, he was honoured by the Government of India with the title of Padma Bhushan for his outstanding work in trade and commerce. He was awarded Lakshya Business Visionary by National Institute of Industrial Engineering, Mumbai, in 2006. The Aligarh Muslim University bestowed on him an honorary degree of Doctorate of Literature, in June 2008 on the 58th Convocation Ceremony of the University.

Receiving Rajiv Gandhi International Award

The Wesleyan University in Middletown, Connecticut, in 2009, awarded an honorary doctorate for his outstanding philanthropic work. The XLRI, Jamshedpur has given him the Sir Jehangir Gandhy Medal for Industrial and Social Peace.

However, the most prestigious award is one that the Government of India bestowed on him, it is the Padma Vibhushan, the second highest civilian award of 2011.

□□□